LET IT BE OVER!

Vanessa R. Byrd

No part of this publication may be reproduced, stored in a retrieval system, or transmitted, in any form, or by any means, electronic, mechanical, photocopying, recording, or otherwise, without the prior consent of the publisher.

The publisher makes no representations or warranties with respect to the accuracy or completeness of the contents of this book and specifically disclaims any implied warranties of merchantability or fitness for a particular purpose. Neither the publisher nor author shall be liable for any loss of profit or any commercial damages.

Unless otherwise indicated, all scripture quotations are taken from The Holy Bible, King James Version © 1989 Thomas Nelson, Inc.

Printed in the United States of America.

First Edition

Copyright 2018 Vanessa R. Byrd

ISBN-13: 978-0692154410
ISBN-10: 0692154418

I dedicate this book to my son, Marcus Byrd, my daughter, Lateshia Byrd, and my grandson, "The Baseball Player," Marcus Byrd.

To my church family, Paradise Christian Center, thank you for your love and support.

Thank you, everyone! I love you to life!

Table of Contents

Foreword

Introduction 1

-1- God's Word Empowering Your Mind 3

-2- The Power of a Made-Up Mind 8

-3- Breaking Free 12

-4- Shifting Into Your Purpose 17

-5- Getting Rid of the Old Stuff 22

-6- Released to Elevate 27

-7- Get Ready for the New 33

I Decree and Declare 39

Let It Be Over Today 41

Prevailing Prayer 42

About the Author 43

Foreword

One of the most difficult things to discover in any situation is not necessarily the "what" but the "how." How do I move on once I know I need to move on? How do I get over things once I know I need to get over them?

The average mind will get bogged down at the crossroad between what and how, and will never really command the moment and move forward. They may leave that place in life, without really having conquered the issue, only to have to revisit it in the future. I always say, "You can't command now what you appropriate to a future moment." If you want to take command over it now, you'll have to deal with it now!

In the material you now hold, there are some powerful keys to both the whats and the hows of life. Bishop Vanessa R. Byrd has been graced with the capacity to simplify the complicated and make plain an understanding of the mechanisms and mechanics of progressing in life!

Keys, however, only work if you put them in the lock and TURN them. Information and revelation are keys that only work if you allow them to turn you!

Bishop Demetrius J. Sinegal, Ph.D.
Senior Pastor
The Kingdom Church of Houston, TX

*"Keys, however, only work if you put them in the lock and TURN them.
Information and revelation are keys that only work if you allow them to turn you!"*

Introduction

All of us have had moments when we were tested beyond our comfort zone. This is not an easy place to be. We have been in situations where we were looking for quick fixes from God. However, there is a blessing tucked away in every experience God allows us to go through. I am reminded, in the Word of God, according to Romans 9:28 "For He will finish the work and cut **'it'** short in righteousness…" At this point, we could either press forward past the pain, or turn back to our comfort zone holding on to the **"it"** in our lives. No matter what our **"it"** may be: whether it's overcoming obstacles, past relationships, poverty, unholy soul ties, or identity crisis, God can deliver us out of them all as long as we don't stand in His way.

How are we getting in God's way? We are standing in God's way when He is trying to prove Himself in our lives. We are allowing problems and issues to take control over our lives. We find ourselves holding on to baggage that we don't need. God is elevating us to another place. We must trust God to strengthen us not only to let **"it"** go, but to make a conscious decision to **"let it be over."** We have to give our "It" an expiration date. Better yet, we have to give the benediction to it with an "Amen." When we say "Amen," that means it is done, it is final, the end! God will conclude His dealings concerning our lives completely and without delay.

We need a divine Word from God that can shift our lives to a greater place of purpose. We don't need a cliché for what we are going through. We need the wisdom of God that will lead us into the mindset of staying focused on our purpose. We must not allow anything or anyone to make us miss our opportunity with God.

Sometimes it's hard to let things go, but we have to prevail over whatever it is and trust God. Many things have occurred in our lives to bring us to a greater place. In the midst of it all, we must understand that we have to go through certain things and know that everything has a season. Just as we know that there's an end to every chapter in a book, we must live with the understanding that there is an end to what we are going through.

I DECREE an opening of spiritual ears to hear the direction and guidance of the Holy Spirit. I DECREE freedom from every source of depression, oppression and suppression in the name of Jesus that we may be released to elevate in God.

After reading this book, you will be able to give the benediction to your issues, and you will be empowered to **"Let It Be Over"**!

-1-
God's Word Empowering Your Mind

"So shall My word be that goeth forth out of My mouth; it shall not return unto Me void, but it shall accomplish that which I please, and it shall prosper in the thing whereto I sent it." - Isaiah 55:11

The Word of God is very important. Power comes from the word when we hear it. The word will teach, guide and strengthen us. Therefore, it is our responsibility to take the Word of God and shift it from our minds into our hearts. Every day we wake up, we are faced with many decisions. We must not allow negative thoughts and destructive decisions to pull us out of the will of God. When we act on God's Word, our lives will be full of peace, joy, love, power and great deliverance. *Psalms 107:20* says, *"God sent forth His word and healed them and delivered them from their destruction."*

"For the Word of God is quick, and powerful, and sharper than any two-edged sword." - Hebrews 4:12

We live our lives as if it takes God all day to do things. The Word of God is living. It is active and it cuts through anything that blocks our minds. All we have to do is trust God. Once we give our situations and problems to Him, we should believe that He is going to do what we asked Him to do. I challenge you to take a faith walk. Put it in God's hands and watch Him destroy our enemies.

"Is not My word like as a fire? Saith the Lord; and like a hammer that breaketh the rock in pieces?" - Jeremiah 23:29

God's word has power to those who believe. If we need something burned up or broken, we should give it to God. There is nothing too big or too hard for God.

"Thy word is a lamp unto my feet and a light unto my path." - Psalm 119:105

If we need guidance, all we have to do is ask God. He left us a road map, His word. He will send us to the right place and show us the right thing to do. We must have a relationship with Him, so that when we hear His voice we won't ignore it.

"And be not conformed to this world: but be ye transformed by the renewing of your mind, that ye may prove that good, and acceptable, and perfect, will of God." - Romans 12:2

The world offers us its own way of dealing with issues, but this is only a temporary fix. God wants to offer us complete deliverance. In order to be free we must let go of the world's way and accept what God says in His word.

God has experience of how powerful His word is.
"By the word of the Lord, were the heavens made; and all the host of them by the breath of His mouth." - Psalms 33:6

God's word has not failed Him yet. After creating the world we live in, the Word of God has survived thousands of years and is still coming true. Everything we see, feel, smell, taste and hear is a result of His word.

> *"Study to show thyself approved unto God, a workman that needeth not to be ashamed, rightly dividing the word of truth." - 2 Timothy 2:15*

All we have to do is read and study the word and believe that it is truth. Once we know the truth, the truth will make us free and will begin to work in our lives.

"Bring truth to your mind."

"Let this mind be in you which was also in Christ Jesus." - Philippians 2:5

If it was good enough for Christ Jesus, it is good enough for us. Christ lived His whole life being obedient to God. As a result, He was able to fulfill His purpose. Jesus had all kinds of tests and trials, but God delivered Him out of them all. He is our example. We do not have to accept the seeds the devil is planting in our mind. We can be **free.**

A mind can be a dangerous thing. It's the leader of our actions. Our actions are a direct result of our thoughts. If the mind were to die, the body would have no movement. In order to stay focused, we must reset our mind. When our mind is clear and free, we can change our circumstances. Things that happened today will not attach themselves to our tomorrow.

The mind is a battlefield. We are engaged in a constant conflict between the mind of the flesh and the mind of the spirit. When we are spiritually renewed, we come to understand that we cannot have a positive life and a negative mind. The enemy knows the tremendous power of our mind. He understands that it is the main decision-making source and the puppet master of our body.

This is why he tries to capture it for himself. The enemy knows that if he can control our thoughts, he can control our actions.

The enemy will attempt to set up "strongholds" against us. It is important to guard the gates of our minds. If we don't have a clear mind on a particular issue, we will not develop in that area spiritually. When we are positive thinkers, we will have successful living. When I go through tough times, I am reminded not to worry because God has equipped me to go through it. We all have encountered situations where we were asked to do something that was challenging. It may seem as if we can't do it; but we can when we put our mind to it. According to Philippians 4:13, *"We can do all things through Christ that strengthens us."*

Things will happen in our lives that are beyond our control. No matter what challenges comes our way, I believe that God has orchestrated them to push us to our greater. We must understand that before God can introduce us to greater, we must be tried. The Word of God states in Job 23:10, *"He knows the way that we should take, and when we are tried,* **then** *we will come out as pure gold."* Our minds have to be tried and challenged so that God can see the real intent of our hearts. So, if our minds are in the right place, in God, we will have the ability to overcome any challenge that presents itself to us.

"Our Mind is a fantastic gift; it is a creative force of power."

A carnal mind is death, but the spiritual mind is life. Our inner man (mindset) is constantly changing. We are being transformed by the renewing of our mind when we are living by the spirit and not the flesh. The eighth chapter of Romans teaches us that if we "mind" the things of the flesh, we will walk in the flesh; but if we "mind" the things of the spirit, we will walk in the spirit.

"Therefore if any man be in Christ, he is a new creature: old things are passed away; behold, all things are become new."
- 2 Corinthians 5:17

When we accept Christ in our lives, everything about us becomes new. It becomes our spiritual birthday. We no longer wear the same clothes or the same shoes. We've got a new look, a new walk, and a new talk. Now we belong to Christ and no longer listen to the devil. He made us a promise in Isaiah 26:3a, "Thou will keep him in perfect peace, whose mind is stayed on thee." It takes determination, but we can do it.

An assured mindset is having the confidence to move forward, even though whatever is taking place in our lives at the moment is not so good. Expect God to bring the good out of it! Now that we're a new person in Christ, we don't have to allow the old things to affect our future. We must be ready to leave behind the evidence of our past. Blessings and favor will approach us when we make the decision to move forward. For Paul says in Philippians 3:13, "Brethren, I count not myself to have apprehended: but this one thing I do, forgetting those things which are behind, and reaching forth unto those things which are before." We shouldn't be afraid to separate ourselves from everything that is not like God. With a new mindset we won't even miss those things. I encourage us to practice being positive in every situation that arises. It's time to press toward our destiny. As God has promised in His word, we can be assured that all things work together for the good!

-2-
The Power of a Made-Up Mind

When we have a made-up mind, nothing will be able to distract us. Nothing will be able to keep us from our freedom in God. Letting go is not only an action, but it's a decision. Once we have made that decision to go all the way in God, no one or nothing will be able to hold us down. There are many reasons why we should operate knowing that we have God's power backing us. There are some things that God wants to manifest in and through us once we arrive at that place. People go through life and they wonder why they are not bearing fruit. They wonder why they are not productive or lack the power to let go of their past. There are many reasons that prohibit us from bearing fruit.

We become frustrated because we know there is so much more God has inside of us that we should be doing. Frustration can cause us to want to give up. Instead, we should allow frustration to bring us into a place of motivation. What we thought couldn't happen should push us into a greater strength to get it done. If we are not frustrated about it, we will not be motivated to do it.

"Frustration is the motivation for our elevation."

When we make up our minds that we will let nothing separate us from the love of God, we will begin to experience elevation in our lives. This is when we will see things manifest at an entirely different level, just because we have made the decision to never turn back. God will begin to fight on our behalf and give us the peace that will surpass all understanding.

When we say today that we have moved forward, we have conquered the frustration. Now that we have made up our minds, we are ready for the elevation, and we will see that our perception (how we see it) and decisions (how we think) have changed.

Focus Point

We know that the enemy targets the mind. If we keep thinking that we are stuck in neutral, we'll believe in our heart that we are stuck and we will find ourselves not moving. #GetIntoDrive

Points to an empowered mind.

- **Read and then meditate on the word. (Joshua 1:8)**

    "This book of the law shall not depart out of thy mouth; but thou shalt meditate therein day and night, that thou mayest observe to do according to all that is written therein: for then thou shalt make thy way prosperous, and then thou shalt have good success."

- **Act on God's word. ((James 1:22)**

    "But be ye doers of the word, and not hearers only, deceiving your own selves."

- **Wait on God. (Isaiah 40:31)**

    But they that wait upon the Lord shall renew their strength; they shall mount up with wings as eagles; they shall run, and not be weary; and they shall walk, and not faint.

Can you get over it? Yes!

- **By acting on God's word (John 15:7)**

    "If ye abide in Me, and My words abide in you, ye shall ask what ye will, and it shall be done unto you."

- **By confessing it, believing it, confronting it and speaking it.**

    The enemy's job is to fight you in your mind. He does that by replaying what happened to you in your mind, but on today I touch and agree with you that you will let it be over by proclaiming it through the Word of God.

Focus Point

According to John 10:10, "The thief cometh not, but for to steal, and to kill, and to destroy: I am come that they might have life, and that they might have it more abundantly."   **#VictoriousThinker**

"And we know that all things work together for the good to them that love God, to them who are the called according to His purpose." - Romans 8:28

Letting go of our past and forgetting it is not a selfish thing, but it's a step closer to our JOY. I encourage you to put God's word into action.

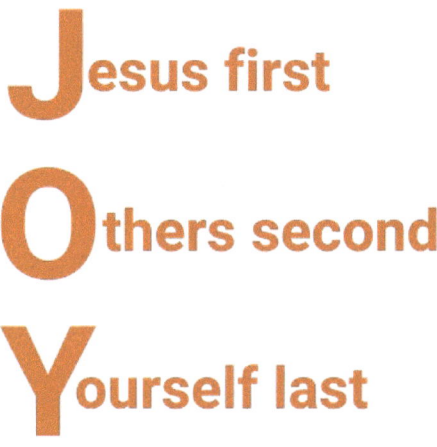

Jesus first

Others second

Yourself last

This is a way of God's glorifying Christ and helping others through us. Positive minds produce positive lives! **#PositiveThinking**

-3-
Breaking Free

We all have encountered moments in our lives where we felt free from our temporary victories, only to find out that we still had shackles on our feet. So we wonder why it is so easy to slide back into defeat. Victory and liberty are obtained when the key to the stronghold is found and destroyed. Once the stronghold is destroyed, it will be like a weight that is lifted off. The power will remain, and we will have the fortitude to move forward instead of repeating the same problem over and over again. If we go in our own power and authority, there is never a real victory. Victory comes when we submit to the power and authority of Christ.

Strongholds are things that grip, hold on to, or take root in our lives. If we don't let things go, we will find ourselves being easily pulled back into a situation that we just left behind. In order to get rid of whatever our "it" may be, the "it" must be cut off at the root so that those issues will no longer be able to grow. Strongholds are Satan's secret weapon. They counteract the will of God in our lives, causing us to be in a place where we struggle to submit.

"Submit yourselves unto God; resist the Devil, and he will flee from you." - James 4:7

We must submit ourselves to God. To submit means to surrender from the inside. When we are obedient from the heart, we will give up the reigns of our lives. Submitting to God gives Him control over our lives.

"For the weapons of our warfare are not carnal, but mighty through God to the pulling down of strongholds; Casting down imaginations, and every high thing that exalteth itself against the knowledge of God, and bringing into captivity every thought to the obedience of Christ." - 2 Corinthians 10:4

We have the power to break the hold of the stronghold, take back our minds, and control our thoughts.

Focus Point

We can hit around the problem, but until the root of that issue is dealt with, we will not have the victory. Victory does not come from measuring the enemy, but from the measurements of submitting to God! **#FromVictimToVictor**

The past is not the past until we have properly dealt with it. To deal with the past we have to be real with ourselves. It is hard to escape from the emotional baggage of abuse, divorce, bullying, abandonment, neglect, trust issues, failed relationships and church hurt. It is important that we do not become pain carriers. Pain carriers hold images of the past captivated into their future.

The things in our past helped play a part in who we are today. It's time to let things go and get over it. The issues of generational sins do not have to be our future. God has given us the power and authority to change that.

When you choose to carry the past, you are making a decision to have a negative influence in your life today.

Letting go of the past releases streams of living water into our lives. It will enable God to do a new work in us. II Corinthians 7:14 says, "If any man be in Christ, he is a new creature; old things are passed away. Behold all things become new." God will bring us into a place to forgive the ones who hurt us. We no longer have to hold on to the things others have done to us. God has given us a new heart and a new mind. This new heart is full of compassion and loving kindness. So now we can do what the Word says, FORGIVE. No matter how difficult it may be, it is something we have to do to be free.

Luke 11:4 says, "Forgive us of our sins, as we also forgive everyone who sins against us."

I've talked about breaking free, dealing with, and letting go of our past. Now here are some tips on how to get over it and move on to bigger, better, larger, greater.

Take responsibility for your own actions.

We always play the blame game, when in reality we have played a big part why things did not go our way. We must repent of our sins. Don't become the victim. We are the victor. We are more than conquerors through Christ which strengthens us.

Strive to do better than the behaviors and past failures that were modeled in the past by our parents.

We should create generational favors instead of generational curses by being obedient to God. We are not our parents. God will hold us accountable for what we have done, not for what our parents did. God knew us before we were formed in our mothers' wombs. We are warriors - not pain carriers. We have different storms for a greater purpose. Our greatness comes from the word. God has a predestined plan for each of us. The only way we are going to discover what that plan is, is by reading and meditating on the word. The word will set us free from past failures and curses. God gives us power to tread over serpents, scorpions and all the power of the enemy (even our mind). With God's help we can separate ourselves from what used to hold us down.

"We are given choices, either we make them according to our past or our future."

If you forgave and you are still emotionally attached to your "It," you did not forget. We must be aware of our emotional baggage. "Let It Be Over." It is easier said than done, but letting it go will keep your mind drama free. Let's not compare our current situation to our past. It could become a hindrance to our future. Forgiveness will set us free from our past faster than holding on to it. Just let it go and let it be over! However, we cannot do it alone. We must learn to look to the hills from which cometh our help according to Psalm 121:1. No matter how long we have been carrying the unforgiveness, God can help. He promised to be a present help in the time of trouble. It does not matter whether the trouble comes from the outside or inside. Nothing is too hard for God. Once our mind begins to focus on God, He promises to keep us in perfect peace.

Learn to forgive and ask for forgiveness!

Focus Point

"Emotional baggage builds up walls, but a peaceful mind, lets it go and allows it to be over." **#FreedomByChoice**

-4-
Shifting Into Your Purpose

Moving forward is proof of spiritual maturity and growth. When it comes down to the testing of our faith, our mind will develop perseverance by reading the word. According to James 1:3-4, perseverance must finish its work so that we may be mature and complete, not lacking anything.

When we are dealing with personal growth, we must start with the word. It will help us to make the right decisions and create great expectations. When we extend forgiveness, we can expect God to strengthen us in areas where we are weak. When we are dealing with spiritual growth, we should start by planting seeds. Where do these seeds come from? They come from reading the word.

In spite of how others have treated us, someone needs our encouragement today. The word tells us to be kind and affectionate towards one another. Get to know your offender. Find the root of the issue and begin to plant a seed into that fertile ground. Then water it every chance you get. This will help encourage them into a better tomorrow.

"Sometimes we have to look beyond our pain to see a reason to pray."

When we were younger and were disciplined by our parents, it stung for a little while, but the pain of yesterday has become a faded memory today. Through growth and remembrance, we will know on tomorrow not to do it again. Remember, if something has caused us pain on yesterday, go to God about it. As a result our faith will grow causing us to be healed today. This will help strengthen us to testify about it tomorrow.

Focus Point

Having faith in God helps us to go from yesterday to tomorrow. Remember, "Jesus is in the center of it all." He is our help today.
#InsuredByFaith

Find Assurance In Trusting Him…

Many of us struggle in certain areas, wondering if it will ever change. According to 2 Corinthians 1:20, "For all the promises of God in him are yea, and in him Amen, unto the glory of God by us. God is going to put us in a position to let go of everything that has been a hindrance to our breakthroughs. All it takes is one good break or idea and we could find ourselves at the top.

It's not by coincidence that things just fall into place. We don't see it coming, but it's how God **is** shifting things in our favor. What we've failed to realize is that when we bear God's name, He can cause an opportunity to find us. All He requires us to do is trust Him. Trust Him when He moves things, people, or situations out of our lives. When our mind becomes focused on the word, it will be easy to trust God for what He is doing. We will be able to leave the past in the past and pursue the future that God has for us.

Some people dislike or are afraid of change. In order to progress in life, we must embrace the new because our old lives have already passed away. We just have to allow "it" to be over. What used to be a struggle is not anymore when we stop reliving the past. God is saying, "Get ready; I'm about to shift things." In order to do so, we have to let go of the dead weight that has been holding us down. It's time to cut it off, **let it be over**, and shift.

Because we bear His name, we are strong and able!

God will not allow anything to keep us from our destiny. We've all faced something from our past hurt that has been coming up against us year after year. It becomes dead weight. That dead weight could be addictions, bad habits, wrong company, brokenness, lost identity, church hurt, or sickness. These are only a few, but let's think about it and name our dead weight. Whatever is holding us back from moving forward, we need to let it go. When God shifts things, they will no longer become our hindrance, but they will push us to a better position in our lives.

God's favor is being released in a new way. This shift is designed to accelerate us and take us beyond any place we could go on our own. Let's encourage one another to stop worrying about our past hurts. Even the things that are trying to hold us back from our destiny are no match for God. They may seem bigger, stronger, or more powerful, but God knows how to shift things around to get us to where we're supposed to be. It may not look like it in the natural, but we serve a supernatural God.

He's about to breathe in our direction in a new way. The enemies we've seen in the past, we will see no more. When we alter our attitude by saying, "God, I believe things are shifting in my favor," that's our letting go of our past and activating our faith. When we say "God I'm ready; I'm taking the limits off You," that is enlarging our vision to overcome what a medical report says is impossible. When we see a wayward child change his mind and get back on the right course, it will encourage us to see the rainbow in the midst of the storm. It will reassure us that there's a purpose at the end of it all.

When we are about to shift into our purpose, God will release the abundance upon us. Our obedience will cause an overflow of blessings to come our way. For example, in Genesis 48:13-20, Manasseh was supposed to be the first born to inherit the blessings of Jacob. When Jacob (Israel) crossed his hand over the heads of his two grandsons, Ephraim, who was the younger son, received the blessing instead. The right hand gave the greater blessing. God is going to cause us to accomplish what we thought would never happen. In this day and time this did not happen. It was the first born who received the blessings. When God is in control, He can do a complete reversal. Ephraim was born second. He wasn't next in line. He didn't qualify for it. He might not have deserved it. But God said, "I'm shifting him to a new position."

God has shifts in our future that will put us in a position that we do not qualify for. We may not be next in line. We may not have seniority. But because we honor God, He will move us up to receive a "double blessing." God will bless us on purpose, elevate us, accelerate our dreams, and give us what we don't deserve.

We serve an awesome God! It's time to trust God to do something new in our lives. Start expecting supernatural favor. We're going to surpass the greatness of man's power into the supernatural greatness of God's favor.

"Therefore if any man be in Christ, he is a new creature: old things are passed away; behold all things are new." – II Corinthians 5:17

Focus Point

"When we move ourselves from our past to our future of opportunities, it causes God to bless us. We're showing Him that we're trusting Him to do it." We must let go of the old things so that we can approach our new with expectancy.
#ExpectingGreater

-5-
Getting Rid of the Old Stuff

Let's imagine we are in a one-bedroom apartment with a growing family. Sooner or later we will start to feel uncomfortable and crowded. We all have friends that hang out, drink, and party, but we no longer live that lifestyle. We tolerate them because we enjoy their company. We may even find ourselves in relationships where we are being mistreated.

These conditions and circumstances make us vulnerable, so we spend our lives either trying to fit in or we end up settling for anything. If we are in a place where we don't feel comfortable or we feel isolated, then we have to do something about it. Everyone wants to feel loved and accepted. For these reasons we are pushed to a willingness to endure. It's time to get out of those unhealthy relationships and cut all ties. It's time to be concerned about our long-term future and not our short-term past. We have to get to the point where we can say, **"I can't stay here; I've got to move."** When we have more bills than money, **"I can't stay here; I've got to move."** When a relationship is not working out, **"I can't stay here; I've got to move."** When we spiritually outgrow where we are, **"I can't stay here; I've got to move."** When we have been lied on, talked about, mistreated, and taken advantage of by our families and friends, **"I can't stay here; I've got to move."** It's time to make that move, because sometimes if we don't make the move ourselves, God will give us a reason for that move to happen. We just have to follow His lead, have faith, and trust in what He's doing.

Proverbs 3:5 says, "Trust in the Lord with all your heart and lean not on your own understanding." We may not understand what God is doing, but we need to get to a place where we know He will not lead us astray. There's a purpose for why we have to move. We are expanding to bigger, better, larger, and greater.

No one likes to pack up and move. We know there is a lot of work to be done and everything can't go with us. Some things we have to throw away because they're old and outdated. Keep in mind these things will not fit into our new place. So when we are in a new place in God, we have to let go of certain habits, certain friends, certain family members, and certain places because they have expired. If they say that we are acting brand new, just say, "Thank you! That's what God intended for us to do."

When you change your atmosphere it changes your outlook!

Focus Point

"Let all things be done decently and in order."
- 1 Corinthians 14:40

The testing of our faith develops perseverance by:
- Keeping God first in our life
- Saying no to temptations
- Revoking all visitation rights of sin
- Operating with a forgiving heart
- Trusting in God's guidance

"God is getting ready to change our status." **#BrandNew**

Now that we've reached our moving day, it's time to get rid of some stuff. We hold onto things because they have sentimental value. Those values can be a hindrance to our moving forward. We have to throw away everything that has expired. We cannot operate with stale faith. According to Isaiah 43:19, "Behold, I will do a new thing; now it shall spring forth." We have been upgraded!

When we restore our computer, everything that didn't come from the factory with the system disappears. Only what was originally on the computer remains. The same thing happens with us. When God restores us, He cleans us up and gives us an upgrade. Once we have been upgraded, we are saved from corruption.

Some of us hide things away in boxes (our hearts) and put them in storage (our minds) so that when we feel the urge to go back to it again, we have easy access. That's why it is a good idea to throw away things that we don't need so that we will not go back to them again.

Focus Point

"God is about to cause a defragmentation of your mind."
#LetHimUpgradeYou

The move has taken place. Now we are ready to clean up the old place, making sure it is left in good condition. Say goodbye and close the door. II Corinthians 5:17 says, "Therefore if any man be in Christ, he is a new creature: old things are passed away; behold, all things become new."

When we go to funerals, we go to say goodbye to our loved ones. We're going to miss them, and we realize we will never see them again. However, through time we heal and it doesn't hurt as much. The same thing happens when we belong to God and we allow His word to comfort us in day to day problems. The word will heal, restore and strengthen us. Then we will be able to experience the joy many people feel when a child is born. Instead of crying, we will be glad and joy will fill our empty spaces. Life before the child was born is remembered no more.

We have to tell our past goodbye and give God an invitation to our future. It's time to say goodbye to abuse, temporary fixes, friends who mean us no good, bad attitudes, unwanted negativity, and everything that is not of God. Just take a moment to say hello to love, joy, and peace. Then embrace God's wisdom.

When we give our issues the benediction, we say, "God, You're invited into my heart." We tell God to walk with us in every situation. We acknowledge the Holy Spirit and give him the chance to lead and guide us.

There's nothing like being set free and forgetting all those things that held us back in the past. Issues are our past, Jesus is our present, and God is our future. No matter how things were in the beginning for us, it is our desire to be caught up in the air to meet God. Heaven is our reward. Everything we have gone through was a distraction to knock us off course. The enemy didn't know we were going to get a word that would change our thinking and give us victory.

"Chaos may have been our beginning, but it does not have to be our ending."
#RestoreRefreshRenew

Focus Point

"Forget about your problems; God is getting ready to manifest your promise." **#GreatExpectations**

-6-
Released to Elevate

Many of us have been through some things that we are too embarrassed to speak about. Some of those things were beyond our control; other things came from poor choices that we've made. But through it all, the bad happened to bring the good out of us.

Even with the mistakes we have made, we can use the lessons we learned as stepping stones to our now. We have to have a mindset that looks at everything and says, "Wow, my past was not a mistake." Our past has given us wisdom. Our past has given us an avenue into a better future. Our past also has given us courage and strength for the next trial.

There are some people watching us as we go through the fire. They are waiting to see how the story ends. They are looking to see if we are the examples they can follow. The attacks can be painful and bring destruction. However, we know things don't have to always turn out bad. According to Psalms 119:71, "It is good for me that I have been afflicted; that I might learn thy statutes." In the end, it's all about how we handled that situation.

God will not put more on us than we can bear, nor will He leave us to face it alone. The past experience may have hurt us, upset us, or made us feel worthless, but it was working for our good. It had to happen to us. Our testimonies had to come from somewhere.

"And we know that all things work together for good to them that love God, to them who are the called according to His purpose." - Romans 8:28

People catch our attitude like they catch a cold. It's contagious. We must be aware of what we're passing on. We are more influential than we think! We can't get mad at the past that helped shape us and we can't hold onto it. Why? Because it has the potential to break us if we are not careful.

Focus Point

Some people will hold our past over our heads like a halo, but we do not have to revert back to who they say we were. We must walk with our heads up and be who God says we are now!
Be alert; don't revert!

"Don't allow the enemy to accuse you of a sin that God has forgiven you of." **#PastFree**

Did you know that your faith can change the way your mind sees things? Faith is so powerful and wonderful that it can actually change our reality. We can look at a situation in our lives and begin to speak the Word of God over that situation and because of our faith, that situation will change. If we would listen to what God says in His word, it will increase our faith. For example, according to the

Word of God, if we are poor, we can become rich by speaking faith over our lives.

Faith is having the ability to look at what is real and begin to speak a new reality into existence. Proverbs 18:21 says, "Death and life are in the power of the tongue: and they that love it shall eat the fruit thereof." We have to be careful how we speak over our lives. Faith gives us the strength to always have in our mind that God is able to do exceeding abundantly above all that we ask or think because God is just that good! It's time out for speaking death over our situations; we are supposed to speak life. If we had not gone through our difficult issues, we would not be who we are today. We are more than conquerors. We are rich with God's Glory. We are blessed and highly favored. We are who we believe ourselves to be.

"Power and authority are exercised through our words."

We generally make promises with the intention of keeping those promises. However, circumstances may arise that are beyond our control, and they may prevent us from keeping the promises. God has the authority, the ability and the power to make and keep every covenant, every promise, every word that He speaks. He has the power to make it our reality. According to Isaiah 55:11, "So shall My word be that goeth forth out of My mouth: it shall not return unto Me void, but it shall accomplish that which I please, and it shall prosper in the thing whereto I sent it." He may not always give us a quick answer to every problem. God wants to build our faith. God will act on behalf of those who wait for him. So in our waiting, we should believe that we are blessed, because we are! We must become what we believe.

Focus Point

Patience is a virtue. Your waiting is not in vain. God says, "I am working while you are in your waiting."
#BecomeWhatYouBelieve

The choices we make reveal our character. The book of 1 Samuel is full of good and bad choices. Hannah is my focus for this particular subject because not only was she an overcomer but she also had a winning attitude.

Hannah was a woman who was unable to have children. She shared her husband Elkanah with another woman named Peninnah. Elkanah's heart belonged to Hannah, but Peninnah was the only one who could give him children.

Peninnah poked fun at Hannah for not being able to please her husband in a way that she could. We all have been in situations where we had to deal with a Peninnah spirit. God equips us to be overcomers. 2 Corinthians 2:14 says, "Now thanks be unto God, which always causes us to triumph".

"A hardened heart has no room for forgiveness, but a soft heart activates grace."

Hannah chose to cry out to God for what she needed. She had faith in God to step into her situation. God heard her prayer and granted Hannah a son, Samuel.

Some of us make bad choices by retaliating, giving the silent treatment, or holding a grudge. We cannot move ahead with all that baggage; we have to let those things go and seek God's face like Hannah did. God puts us in those predicaments so that He can get the glory. No matter what title we hold or how rich we may be, God will always let us know that we still need Him. In all our situations, Jesus is in the center of it all.

No matter how hard our Peninnah problem may be, we have to deal with it through prayer, worship, and trust in God. When we get out of our feelings and into God's presence, we can and will succeed at becoming an overcomer. When we give our burdens to God, we should leave them at the altar and not pick them up again. Let it be over! We must allow God to give us back our joy again. Like Hannah, we are overcomers because we choose to pray, worship, and trust, God no matter what.

Focus Point

Let's see what God sees. **#FearlessInGod**

Serve your enemy notice!
Look in the mirror and say,

I am a child of the King, and I am made in His image. I am under my Father's protection, so I shall prevail over stress, worry, and struggles in my life.

I am an Overcomer. I will not live in defeat. My Father has given me the power and authority to trample over my enemies. I am blessed and highly favored.

Caution: Be careful how You pursue me.

In Jesus Name!

-7-
Get Ready for the New

Now that our past is behind us, we should feel lighter than before. Now it's time to get ready for the next. Our next becomes our new. We know the feeling we have when we get something new. It has a new smell, a new look, a new touch, and a new feel. It makes us feel good to know that what we went through paid off in the end. The same thing happens in our spiritual lives. What we go through helps us to get restored, refreshed, and revived. That means we have a new attitude, a new mindset, a new praise, a new worship, and new faith.

When God gives us that finishing grace, it doesn't take a lot to change things. Starting is easy; finishing is what can be difficult. Anyone can have a dream, but it takes determination, perseverance, and a made-up mind to see it come to pass. So now that we are in our new, we have to work twice as hard to stay there. If God has given us the grace to start, He's also giving us the grace to finish. According to Philippians 1:6, being confident of this very thing, that He which has begun a good work in you will perform it until the day of Jesus Christ.

"We were not created to give up, quit, or to throw in the towel. We were created to finish!"

At times, we can feel so burdened down with negative things. We don't have a chance to see ourselves for who we are in God. It's time to evaluate our spiritual self-image. In order to evaluate our self-image, we have to ask ourselves, "What are my motives?" We have to be real with ourselves. We have to make sure we are aware of what we are doing that's not of God.

A healthy self-image shows us how to let God hold us up when others put us down. We are the vessels that God trusted to go through to build us up spiritually. We will see it as a blessing and an honor for God to use us in such a way that He can bring His people closer to Him. Now that we understand what God is doing in our lives, we should be able to release the anger, pain, loneliness, resentments and feelings of punishment. There's freedom in our release. God is glorified in our deliverance. Now that we are free, we are ready to elevate in God.

Focus Point

"A healthy spiritual self-image gives us freedom to elevate in God."

God has given us the outlet of release we need to soar.

Isaiah 40:30 - "But they that wait upon the Lord shall renew their strength; they shall mount up with wings as eagles; they shall run, and not be weary; and they shall walk, and not faint."
#ReleasedToSoar

Now that we are released to elevate, it's time to pursue our opportunity to do what God has called us to do. There's no excuse now because we no longer carry unwanted baggage. We realize that our past baggage came with a price, but Jesus paid it all. When we let go and **let it be over**, God will put us in a position to receive. When opportunity knocks at our door, we will be ready to pursue it.

Doesn't it feel good to know that we are set free from all that bondage and we can continue to travel light to our next destination? It's exciting to see what God has for us now that we have been released from bondage. We can be sure that God has something awesome waiting in the balance because of our obedience. It may have been rough. There may have been some things that we did not want to do. Now we know that all of these things led up to our elevation. Let's not miss what God is saying by listening to other people. God will bring His promises to pass when we obey Him. Obedience is better than sacrifice. If we keep doing what God wants us to do we will be successful.

"This book of the law shall not depart out of my mouth, but thou shall meditate therein day and night, that thou mayest observe to do according to all that is written therein: for then thou shall make thy way prosperous, and thou shalt have good success." – Joshua 1:8

"Doors are a symbol of opportunities with open access to our future!"

Focus Point

When we build a relationship with the connector, there are many opportunities and benefits that come along with it. When we build a relationship with God who is our connector, we can make a connection which will cause opportunities to pursue us.

"Don't just attach to God; get connected."
#FaithfullyConnected

We have been crippled by our past long enough. All of our experiences encouraged us to be strong in the Lord. They helped to develop our faith muscles for our power struggles. When we pray, it's time to believe in what God said that He will do for us.

> **"Faith is essential for a dedicated prayer life. Prayer paints the picture; faith makes it happen."**

God has given us power and authority over our situations. Our vision is much clearer now. We can embrace our breakthroughs without relapsing. The person that used to walk in the room and make us angry, no longer affects us. We can see the positive out of the negative. We are more focused on God and His plans for our lives. We have gained love and respect for others and ourselves. If the grave could not hold Jesus down, our opposition should not hold us down. God has given us the power and authority to take it back. He has given us victory and peace.

Focus Point

"Some people come into our lives for a season, and some come for a lifetime. Never mix seasonal people with lifetime expectations."

When we let go:

"Growth can be painful, change is hurtful, but nothing is more painful than staying in neutral and being stuck in a place we don't belong."

If we can deal with our reality, we can have victorious living. Our righteousness is defined by God. He gives to us according to the amount of His spirit within us. That becomes our reality when we learn to trust Him. No longer will we be bound with something that should be over. In God we are free and can have victorious living! According to 1 John 4:4, "Ye are of God, little children, and have overcome them: because greater is He that is in you, than he that is in the world."

The best way to be free and to have victorious living is to be truthful with ourselves. #BeTransparent!

I Decree and Declare

I decree and declare:

That we will no longer struggle in finding our identity. I declare that we will have freedom from demonic possession for those who are bound. God, You said in your word that You knew who we were when we were in our mother's womb. I believe that when we will know who You are, we will know who we are in You.

I decree and declare:

That broken and struggling marriages are healed and that families will come back together and broken hearts will be mended. The enemy comes in to kill, steal, and destroy. The enemy's visitation rights have been revoked in every household. I declare household salvation, because Father, You said that a family that prays together stays together.

I decree and declare:

That we are healed physically, emotionally, and spiritually. We will escape every dart that the enemy has thrown our way. We bind the spirit of oppression and release joy into the atmosphere, because Father, You said that no weapon that is formed against us shall prosper.

I decree and declare:

That our nation is under your hedge of protection. No hurt, harm or danger will come our way as long as we lean and depend on You to be our strength and guide. We say that the Lord is our Shepherd we shall not want, because Father we believe that there's safety in your presence. We decree that a hedge of protection be around our mind, body, family, finances, and ministry, in the name of Jesus.

I decree and declare:

That we have won the victory. We have won the battle over the enemy. Every opposition thrown our way is just a push to our next. Depression will not have a place in our lives because Father You said that the joy of the Lord is our strength. We are strong in our faith in You.

I decree and declare:

That we will have a heart of forgiveness. We will let things go and let it be over, because Father, You said that You have created in us a clean heart and that You have renewed a right spirit within us. We bind the spirit of unforgiveness and release the spirit of forgiveness, peace, and grace. I count it all done in Jesus name, Amen!

Let It Be Over Today!

Now is the time to decree and declare that you will Let It Be Over!

I Decree & Declare:

_____

_____

_____

_____

_____

_____

_____

_____

_____

And It Is So In JESUS' Name, Amen!!!

Prevailing Prayer

Father, I just want to thank You that we have walked into a place of freedom in You. I thank You that today marks the day that we will walk in total victory. The enemy tried to come up against us and lost, bringing us to a closer place in You. Lord, I pray that we will hold on to our confession that we will never return back to what your power has delivered us out of. Lord, I thank You today that our minds, spirits and bodies are complete and whole. From now on, we will keep You in the center of everything that we do. For it is a known fact, Father, that it's only in You that we all live, breathe, move, and have our being. Because of your blood, we are able to have power over what tried to take us down. I bless You, Father, that our past will no longer hold us down. Sickness won't over take us, and poverty has left. You said in Jeremiah 29:11, "For I know the thoughts I think toward you, thoughts of peace and not of evil, to give you an expected end." Thank You for bringing us into our wealthy place.

About the Author

Bishop Vanessa R. Byrd was born and raised in Williamston, NC. She has one son, Marcus Shawn Byrd (wife, Lateshia W. Byrd) and one grandson, Marcus Shawn Byrd II of Greenville, NC.

Bishop Byrd accepted her call into the ministry in 1989, while she was faithfully serving at Cedar Hill Baptist Church in Williamston, NC during her years of evangelism. She answered the pastoral call and founded Paradise Outreach Ministries in Washington, NC, on July 18, 1999.

In following the earthly ministry of Jesus Christ, who came not to be served but to serve and to give His life as a ransom for many, Bishop Byrd is committed to a lifetime of service. Her ministering is built upon the belief that in the name of Jesus Christ, broken hearts can be healed, the captive can be set free, sight can be restored to the blind, and the oppressed can be liberated.

Through it all, Bishop Byrd acknowledges that if it had not been for the LORD who was on her side, none of this would have been possible, and she bases the success of the ministry upon Jeremiah 29:11, "For I know the thoughts that I think towards you, saith the LORD, thoughts of peace, and not of evil, to give you an expected end."

Because the Favor of GOD is upon her, she will always honor Him by saying, "To GOD Be the Glory for the things that HE has done!"

www.ingramcontent.com/pod-product-compliance
Lightning Source LLC
Chambersburg PA
CBHW041526090426
42736CB00035B/21